# *Becoming a*
# BALLERINA

UNIVERSE

First published in the United States of America in 2003
by UNIVERSE PUBLISHING
A Division of Rizzoli International Publications, Inc.
300 Park Avenue South
New York, NY 10010
www.rizzoliusa.com

© 2003 Nancy Ellison
Text by Susan Jaffe
Design by Opto Design

2004 2005 2006 2007/ 10 9 8 7 6 5 4 3 2

Distributed in the U.S. trade
by St. Martin's Press, New York

Printed in the United States

ISBN: 0-7893-0976-9

Library of Congress Catalog Control Number: 2003104732

# *Becoming a*
# BALLERINA

NANCY ELLISON
SUSAN JAFFE

To Mrs. Fonseca and Mr. Gene
and all of my future students with love.
—Susan Jaffe

To Bill, whose inner child
is my inner child's best friend.
—Nancy Ellison

*Prologue*

This is four-year-old Lexa, who is a ballerina. And a princess.

She got a brand-new blue
tutu and loves to run
around the house dancing!

Port de bras? Second
position? She has years
to perfect her technique.
Right now she dances
only for herself, because
dancing makes her
feel happy.

Alexandra, a promising young ballerina, shows Lexa how to do a plié in first position.

10

With some practice and a
lot of concentration, Lexa
does a great job!

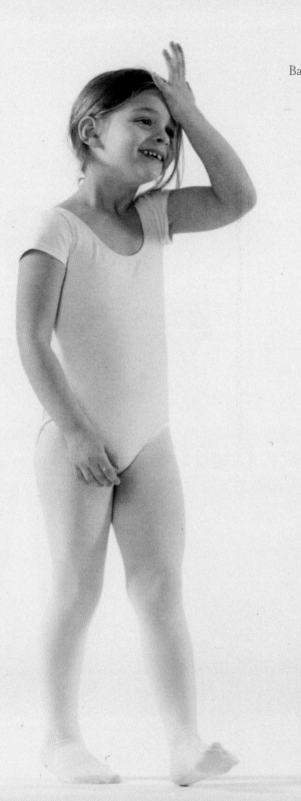

Ballet class is a lot of work!

# Introduction

# *Introduction*

"I am a princess!" I think to myself, running around in my backyard in my mother's silk nightgown. My kingdom—my backyard—hardly offers the rolling hills and castles of my fantasies, but no matter. I raid my mother's jewelry box, wrap my hair in scarves, and race around, lost in my own world until forced to join the real one again for lunch. My mom, perhaps tired of having her silk slips covered in grass stains, asks me if I would like to take a dance class at the YMCA across the street. I would, and happily dress in a black leotard and black tights, pleased to look so grown up. The teacher asks us to create our own dances, to be flowers flowing in the breeze, to be dogs basking in the sun. "Is this what a princess does?" I think, disconsolate. I put off creating the dance and end up in class with no plan—no dance! So I wing it. I turn on my music and prance around, pretending that I have worked hard on my choreography. I get busted, however: We had to show our dance twice! I could hardly bear the embarrassment,

knowing that the teacher and my whole class knew I was a big fake. I felt foolish and awful and knew right then that this was not the princess dancing I had hoped it would be. At the year-end recital I see the ballet class getting ready for their performance. They are so beautiful with their hair back in neat buns, lovely little magenta scarves around their necks. They wear pink tights and pink satin slippers with pretty pink ribbons tied up in a sort of Grecian style that crisscrosses around their ankles. Their dancing is so graceful, so refined. Ballet, I realize, is the way I want to move. It is the dance of princesses. I started classes the following year.

And so it began. My love affair with ballet started with a child's fantasy.

Perhaps that's the *only* way to begin.

# Etiquette, Rules, and Grooming

## *Etiquette, Rules, and Grooming*

# There are three "musts" when it comes to taking a ballet class: Show respect to your teacher; pay attention when your classmates dance; and dress so that neither

your clothes nor your hair interfere with your movements. After dancing at the Y for a few years, I switched to the Maryland School of Ballet, where I learned not only how to dance but the kinds of rules to follow when learning ballet. Mrs. Fonseca, a native of Costa Rica, opened the Maryland School of Ballet with Mr. Gene on St. Elmo Street in Bethesda, Maryland. I loved Mrs. Fonseca and Mr. Gene; they were so much fun to learn from. I don't ever remember being scared of them except when we girls got a little too raucous. Mr. Gene was a great storyteller. I remember his story about a young dancer naively taking her place at the barre before the Grand Ballerina arrived for class. The Grand Ballerina is the most important ballerina of all, remember. The other dancers giggled under their breath as the ballerina walked

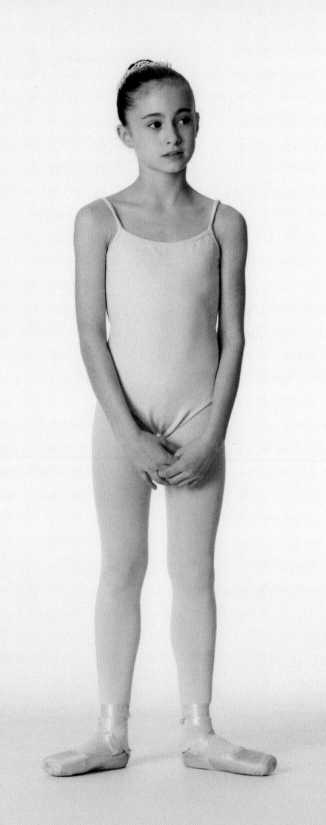

into the room to find her usual spot had been taken by this new, young girl, waiting to see how the ballerina would handle it. With raised eyebrows, the ballerina walked over to the young dancer, looked her up and down and asked for her name. The young dancer suddenly understood that she was in the wrong place. "Would you like to stand here?" the young girl asked. "Why yes, darling, that would be nice," the ballerina replied as she gave a wink to the dancers who were trying to hold in their laughter. Turning bright crimson, the young dancer quickly picked up her dance bag and moved. Yikes! We didn't want that to happen to us! That's how we learned one of the most important rules in ballet class: The young dancers must always show respect to the more advanced ballerinas.

Besides telling us stories, Mr. Gene knew other tricks to get us to pay attention and stay focused. For example, instead of telling us to be quiet, he would explain that when we weren't dancing we could learn from watching our classmates. "If you like what you see," he said, "then try to do the step like that. If you don't like what you see, figure out what is not right about it and try not to make the same mistake. You learn so much by watching." Mrs. Fonseca taught us about how a ballerina should present herself. She always addressed us as "lady." "Lady, please point your feet," or "Lady, that was very good." She wore her long black hair straight back in a high bun and was usually dressed in a black leotard with pink tights, pink slippers, and pink ribbons tied around her ankles. We thought she was so pretty and we all tried to look like her.

At first, my mom was the one in charge of putting my hair up until I was old enough to do it myself. I always became so tense if I saw one hair out of place. "There is a lump!" I would scream, "Mommy, please do my hair again. I can't go to class looking like this!" My hair had to be pulled back so tight that the outer corner of my eyes slanted upward. I had a variety of silk flowers that I would wrap around my bun and I had to be able to see those flowers when I looked straight at myself in the mirror or else I would have to take it all out and start all over again. Sometimes, on bad-hair days after trying several times, I would get so frustrated that I would eventually settle for less than perfect. It took many years until I could become a little more relaxed about my hair.

As for our outfits, we always bought our leotards from Mr. Mac at his store, Artistic. It was right around the corner from our school and we liked hanging out there in our free time, going through our wish lists. Mr. Mac was our favorite supplier of shoes, leotards, leg warmers, tights, and skirts. He was an expert, and his store was full of the latest fashions in the dance world. When we got older, Mrs. Fonseca would let us wear any color leotard we wished and leg warmers if they weren't too bulky. There was always a frenzy of girls rushing to Mr. Mac's place to pick the latest greatest color and newest fashion in leotards, leg warmers, and ballet skirts. If one of us came in one day with a new color leotard, you could be sure that by the end of the week at least half the class would be wearing that same color. Every year Mr. Mac would put out his own catalogue with all of his fashions from the store. I felt so lucky because for a few years, I was one of the models in his catalogue, and for payment Mr. Mac let me keep all of the leotards that I wore the day of the shoot.

What more could a young ballerina want?

Young ballerinas should stick to the basics when it comes to choosing their outfits. Pink or black leotards, pink tights, and pink shoes are always appropriate. Dancers wear clothes like leotards and tights so that they can move freely without anything getting in the way. Later, your teacher might let you play with funky colors and trendy leg warmers, but remember to keep your focus on the dancing!

To prepare for class, Alexandra puts an elastic band around her hair and gathers it into a ponytail. Then she twists her hair into a bun, securing it with bobby pins. Finally, she puts a hairnet on the bun so that her hair stays neat and secure—she does not want any wisps to fly out when she's dancing.

There are many different hairdos that ballerinas need to master so that when they go onstage, they look beautiful: the low bun, the high bun, and what we call "the classical." The classical, used for romantic ballets like *Giselle* and *La Sylphide*, is a high bun with the front of the hair over the ears sort of in an old-fashioned way. Ballerinas should never have messy hair—they are the instruments of fairy tales!

There is a specific etiquette in ballet class that every dancer needs to respect. It is impolite to interrupt the teacher. If you have a question about something that the teacher demonstrates, the question should be asked after the music stops. And always, always, always raise your hand before you speak! Dancing takes concentration, so you should never talk while your classmates take their turns dancing. My teacher said that you can learn a lot about the mistakes that you do not want to make by seeing your classmates make them. You can also improve your own dancing by trying to follow the things your classmates do beautifully.

# Before Class Starts

## Before Class Starts

There is something so fun about the ritual of stretching before class. It is a good time to get to know each other, make new friends, and check out what everybody is wearing. In my classes, we did the "frog" with each other, lying on the floor on our stomachs and bending our legs with our knees and ankles still touching the ground. It's not easy keeping your ankles on the ground: Some of the girls asked their friends to gently push their ankles down to the floor to get a deeper stretch. We did this to improve our turnouts. The turnout is important in every movement of the ballet—it's when your legs are turned out, not just your feet. The perfect turnout should start at your hips; your knees should face the same direction as your toes. Some of the girls wanted a better turnout so badly that they would try to fall asleep at night on their backs in the frog position with books holding their legs down! We talked about how crazy that was, but I know we all tried it.

We got to ballet school early to stretch on the blue-carpeted lobby—that is, to stretch, to talk, and to watch the big girls come in for class. We worshipped one girl in particular: Cheryl. She was very pretty, with brown hair and the most beautiful, slender long legs—perfect for ballet. One day she walked into the school with her leotard cut in the back and tucked down to show more skin. She said it was more comfortable and gave a better line. We all thought that was so cool that within the week, everyone had cut every single leotard they owned to make a lower back. It took a little convincing to get our parents to understand that it was very important to cut our leotards so they fit just how we wanted them and created a better line. That beautiful line was what we longed for, as much as we longed for Cheryl's sense of style. That's because a great line means that the entire body stretches perfectly to execute a movement, making every single position more beautiful.

So we stretched and stretched: front splits, side splits, all splits. We stretched while standing, pulling our legs up to our ears, or lifting our leg behind us while trying to touch our heads. We couldn't do the big stretches until we were warmed up because our teachers told us that it wasn't good to stretch if you weren't warm. So at the end of every warm-up at the barre, our teacher gave us a stretch exercise while the pianist played something pretty and lyrical on the piano. The more flexible and strong the dancer is, the better. So I stretched.

Before class is a good time to prepare your ballet slippers. Your slippers may be canvas, leather, or satin and when you first get them, they should be a little tight—they'll stretch. Girls with very small feet (or very young feet!) might have slippers with the elastics already sewn in place, but with larger sizes the elastics come separately so that you can make sure that the slipper fits perfectly. The elastics should be attached right in front of your ankle and the string that runs through the top of the slipper should be adjusted so that your toes feel comfortable.

31

Alexandra is doing the "frog," just like I used to do before class to make my turnout better. You lie on the floor on your stomach and bend your legs with your knees and ankles still touching the ground. Sound tricky? You can always ask a friend to gently push your ankles down to the floor if they keep flying up.

The point of stretching
is to prepare your body for
dancing and to prevent
injuries. So if you feel
pain, take it easy—take your
stretch as far as you can
and then relax into it—see
how long you can hold it.
Dancers stretch all the time
to keep their muscles
loose. They stretch before
class, after class, in
between rehearsals...

34

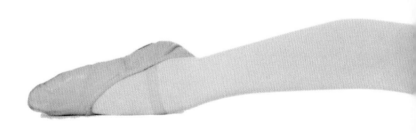

BECOMING A BALLERINA

...and then they stretch some more!

# Learning Positions

## *Learning Positions*

"Okay, everyone. Hold in your stomachs—then let them out. Now hold them in, and let them relax and stick out. Hold them in, let them go, hold them in!" On and on and back and forth, we held our stomachs the correct way: tightly tucked in, back straight, chin up. Then we purposely stuck them out, letting our backs slouch and our bellies fill with air. Mr. Gene always made learning fun. When we practiced the positions, he asked us whether or not we liked how we looked—and how we could make those positions look better. I have such wonderful memories of learning all the positions in the center of the room and all of the subtleties that go with them. Like the difference in the way you hold the body when you are facing straight to the front of the room, or when your body is slightly turned and your arms are over your head in various positions. But first, the basics.

There are five positions of the feet. First position is when the heels are touching each other and both feet are turned out with each toe facing the sides of the room. Second position is the same as first except that there is about a foot-length gap between your feet. In fourth position, your feet should be about one foot apart, with the right foot opposite and in front of the left foot. Fifth position is when both feet are turned out and one foot is directly in front of the other but your feet are touching heel to toe. Third position is like fifth but instead of heel to toe, the heel of your right foot should be touching the arch of your left foot. (Sound complicated? Alexandra demonstrates each of the five positions on pages 42 and 43.)

Equally important are the basic positions of the arms. The first arm position that you learn is called first position *en bas*. In this position, your arms curve in a rounded shape, held close to your body. Your elbows should be lifted, and your pinky fingers should touch the tops of your thighs. Your fingers stretch toward each other and almost touch. Next is *en avant*, sometimes called first position. The term translates to "movement directed forward" and is when you raise your arms to the same level as your belly button (still keeping your arms rounded and your fingers still almost touching). If your teacher says *en haut* she means that you should hold one or both arms above your head.

The positions aren't something that you learn once and then forget about. It takes a long time to master the five positions. Every dancer, from beginner to prima ballerina, practices the five positions at the barre every day. The five positions began with France's Louis XIV, the Sun King. He was a great dancer and he loved his legs—which the five positions showed off just beautifully! To execute the five positions perfectly takes many years of practice. It's the refined adjustments that make all the difference.

There's more! Second position of the arms is when your arms are open and directly stretched out to each side of the body at the level of the breast. For third position, stretch both arms forward, in front of the body and hold one arm above the other. Lastly, fourth position is when the arms are extended with one arm stretched to the front and the other stretched to the back. Your front arm should be crossing the body when you are facing the corner or side of the room.

Learning the positions isn't too tough—perfecting them is. And so I'm grateful to Mr. Gene for encouraging us to make each position as beautiful as possible, something that I now encourage my own students to do. I also always smile at the sight of little girls with their stomachs stuck out!

These are the five basic positions for your feet in ballet. From left to right, Alexandra demonstrates first, second, third, fourth, and fifth positions.

**second**

Everything is the same as first position, except the feet should be about a foot apart.

**third**

Your legs should still be open outward from the hips, but this time the heel of your right foot should be touching the arch of your left foot.

**first**

The heels should touch and the legs should open out from the hips so that the feet make a nice, straight line.

## fifth

The heel of your right foot should be in front of the big toe on the left foot. Your feet should touch, and keep those knees straight!

## fourth

A lot like third position, but your feet should be about one foot apart with the right foot opposite the left foot and in front of it.

BECOMING A BALLERINA

44

Because ballet's inventor, Louis XIV, was French, so are a lot of ballet's terms. Here are several port de bras, which means "carriage of the arms." The way that you hold your arms and hands is just as important as how you do the five positions of the feet. If you look closely, you'll notice how elegantly Alexandra holds her hands. When you dance, your hands should flow energy away from your body—your fingers should never be stiff or awkward. In ballet, every muscle and gesture is important.

45

Your arms complete the line of your body and help you to balance. How you hold them matters for every movement. Here, Alexandra is keeping her elbows open—her arms frame her face beautifully!

# Class Work

## Class Work

Class is a place to sculpt your body and improve your technique. I loved class when I was a child, and I loved it throughout my career. Mrs. Fonseca would be very sweet as she corrected us, but she was also very exact. We loved watching her muscles when she demonstrated positions and combinations. She took us very slowly through each step, showing us what made it wrong or right. Sometimes she would ask one of us to demonstrate and I always felt so honored when I was chosen to show the combination.

The most important element of ballet class is the music—there must always be music playing—so dancers can learn how to truly be the music. One time, Mrs. Fonseca took all of us to Costa Rica to perform. We went to this very old space to rehearse with one of her old teachers who spoke no English and walked with a cane. But he got us to understand him anyway! To make us feel the beat, he stamped his cane on the ground: *uno!* BANG, *dos!* BANG, *tres!*,

Practicing at the barre
is a part of every dancer's
daily routine. The barre
helps you to achieve correct
body placement without
having to worry about bal-
ancing the weight of your
body at the same time.

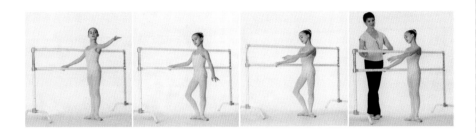

Above, Alexandra uses the barre to help her keep her spine very, very straight while she does a demi-plié in first position. The plié is the first exercise at the barre and one of the most important—it's the basis for everything that dancers do in ballet!

BANG, *cuatro!* BANG. We were so startled by the noise that we could hardly keep from laughing—but we were also afraid of him so we tried to be as quiet as possible. Every once in a while he would poke somebody with that cane as if to tell them to pull up more. And we certainly got the beat!

Class usually follows the same structure, no matter the country, age group, or level. First there is the warm-up at the barre, which lasts about forty-five minutes. Most teachers like to start slowly with pliés and tendus, gradually making the combinations faster and more strenuous as the barre segment progresses. Then the class will move to the middle of the floor to do what's called center work, which focuses a bit more on control and precision. Finally, there's the allegro, or fast, portion of class. This is the time to practice moves like jumps and when ballet students get to work on their speed.

Don't be afraid to try difficult positions and combinations in class. I was always so grateful when the teacher corrected me

Practice, practice, practice!
It's more important to
have a clean position than
to try to get your legs to go
up to your ears! Every day,
Alexandra practices the
same positions over and over.

Her main goal right now is to master the fundamentals: Getting her technique perfect right now will make her dancing more beautiful later.

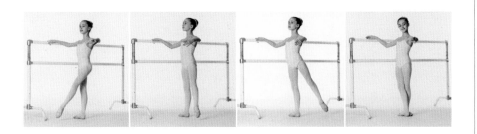

Above, Alexandra practices *ronds de jambe* (circle of the leg), which really helps loosen dancers' hips so that their turnouts are even wider (making every position more lovely!).

because I wanted to know what I needed to correct. I would rather know what is wrong because it's so much easier to correct in class than later on down the road when it becomes a bad habit that is hard to break. We understood that if the teacher corrected you, the teacher liked you and took an interest in your training. Thank heavens that Mrs. Fonseca didn't use a cane!

Later on, all that practice will help Alexandra raise her legs higher off the floor and she'll be able to lift them more easily.

Class takes place in the same order whether you're ten years old or thirty years old. After about forty-five minutes of warming up at the barre, there's a half-hour of center work that will help you develop your balance and control. For the last half-hour of class, there are jumps and other quick movements to help you improve your speed. Class will always move from slow, or adagio, to fast, or allegro.

The arabesque is in every single ballet ever made! Dancers practice arabesque in the adagio part of class, where they focus on perfecting elongating their bodies. But you can also practice arabesque in the allegro part of class, doing them very fast.

57

Turns of all kinds are practiced in the center.

58

Turns take a long time to master and dancers like Alexandra practice what is called "spotting." Spotting is when you focus on one point in the room and keep your eyes there throughout the turn. It's important to really concentrate on the spot so that you can envision it as you quickly whip your head around.

60

## In Slippers

Long before they can go
on pointe, dancers have to
practice (and practice) their
groundwork until things
like turnout, pointing the
foot, and extending the leg
become second nature.
Your teacher will tell you
when you are ready.

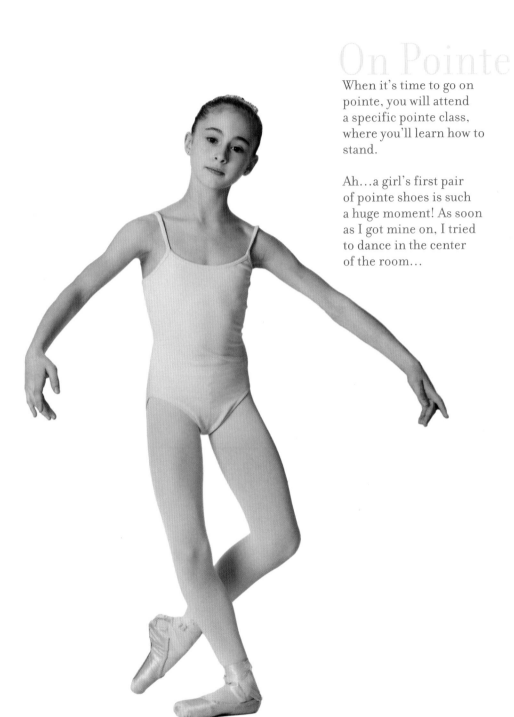

# On Pointe!

When it's time to go on pointe, you will attend a specific pointe class, where you'll learn how to stand.

Ah…a girl's first pair of pointe shoes is such a huge moment! As soon as I got mine on, I tried to dance in the center of the room…

61

…but, like Alexandra,
I should've practiced more
at the barre first! Don't
worry, everybody falls, and
the best thing to do is laugh.

62

CLASS WORK

I spent a lot of time laughing!

It's much safer to practice being on pointe when your teacher is standing right behind you. The barre is also a great way to learn how to stop wobbling. Right now, Alexandra is starting to take pointe class.

64

Later on, if Alexandra becomes a professional dancer, she will wear pointe shoes in all her classes.

CLASS WORK

Alexandra is still very young and is still learning how to do a *grand jeté* (a big throw!). It's the last thing that dancers do in class (it's part of the allegro), and it takes a very long time to perfect. First, the dancer must perfect her arabesque—if you look closely, the jump is a lot like an elongated arabesque in the air. It helps to imagine your favorite dancers (like ABT's Ashley Tuttle) executing a lovely *grand jeté*.

67

But the most important thing about becoming a ballerina—and not a gymnast—is the music. Dancing is the physical form that music takes; music inspires us to dance. Be the music!

# Recital

# Recital

The first dress rehearsal is so exciting! Theaters have a particular atmosphere to them; they even smell different. We found our dressing rooms and started to put on our leg warmers and makeup. Mrs. Fonseca had showed us how to do our makeup so we were anxious to make sure it was perfect. "Darn!" Maya said. "I've done my eyeliner three times already and I still can't get it right." Just like bad-hair days, you can have bad makeup days too.

"Everybody to the stage for a warm-up!" the loudspeaker said. We all giggled as we ran to the stage to see what it looked like. It was a bit chilly onstage and the sidelights were blinding. "Don't look at the lights," Mr. Gene said. "Try to find a spot farther away so that you can keep your balance. It takes a little while to get used to it." I looked out into the pitch-black of the audience. "See that little red light out there in the back of the audience?" Mr. Gene said. "It's your spotting light and it is directly center so you will be

able to find center stage without looking for the white center spot on the floor." "Where is the white center spot on the floor?" Maya asked. "See that tape made into a crisscross that looks like a star over there? Everybody listen up." Everybody huddled around Mr. Gene so that he could explain all the little tricks of the stage.

It was my first performance ever and I was chosen to dance one of the six butterflies in *The Coronation of the Dragonfly Queen*. Mrs. Fonseca did most of the costumes herself with some help from the mothers. The costume shop was in the basement of her house and all the dancers would go there to get fitted. Her basement was full of materials: Shiny sequins, ruffles, and diamond tiaras filled every corner of the room, along with tutus and piles of material, thimbles, and pins. I was overjoyed to see my costume. It was a yellow tutu with shiny, laced borders and there were real wings attached! They were large with a wire spine and some sort of see-through stretch material painted as colorful wings. I felt so special as I pulled that tutu on. I loved the way I looked. I looked like a real ballerina! Mrs. Fonseca adjusted the tutu with pins and said, "Okay, lady. Your costume will look very beautiful on you."

After our warm-up, it was time to get into our costumes and come back to the stage. My feet were hurting: we had rehearsed

many hours and my feet weren't used to it. I cringed as I walked. "Thank God this is only a dress rehearsal today. I don't think I would make it otherwise," I said as Maya and I climbed the stairs that led to the stage. But practicing the steps of the ballet is only half of the battle. Performing is the heart of ballet and it requires more than costumes and technical proficiency. The audience—and your relationship with the audience—is one of ballet's toughest and most rewarding challenges. It's your responsibility to tell the audience a story and to do that, you must know the character as well as you know yourself. Find out what's going on with this character: How does she play a role in her world? Who is she? What does she

Getting the jitters before going on stage is normal and, for many dancers, useful. All of that adrenaline helps dancers to focus. You can use those butterflies to make your performance even better!

74

want? For that matter, what do all of the characters want? Empathize with her; become her: How would you behave in her situation? What would you feel? It's not about the perfect arabesque; it's who you are in this arabesque. Your goal—every ballerina's goal—is to make the audience understand the ballet not just with your outer work, but also with your inner work.

Although I've been onstage countless times after *The Coronation of the Dragonfly Queen*, the thrill of performing never fades. I've always liked to go to the stage fifteen minutes before the show begins to put on my pointe shoes and try a few moves. Then it's show time: The curtain goes up, the lights go out—everybody is in expectation, you can hear the curtain rise. The music starts, the lights go on, and the adrenaline hits. Now is the moment that you rush on the stage—the rest is an act of faith.

Later on, there might be praise from the *New York Times* dance critic or roses presented during the curtain call…

RECITAL

...but right now a hug
from Mom and Dad
is good enough.

BECOMING A BALLERINA

78

RECITAL

*Dreaming…*

*Dreaming…*

# Never underestimate the power of your dreams. They can come true if they are right for you—and if you want them passionately enough. Ballet is one of the most beautiful and fulfilling professions. Yes, it's difficult, but it wouldn't be as fulfilling if it came easily. Ballet is a profession that takes your heart, your mind, your body, and your spirit.

Alexandra Dobles loves ballet and wants someday to be a professional ballerina. She works hard, sometimes attending classes as many as six days a week, participating in the American Ballet Theatre's Summer Intensive Program, and even practicing things like jumps in her free time at home and after hours in the studio. She dreams of becoming one of the ABT's stars, perhaps performing a pas de deux with someone like principal dancer Angel Corella or conveying emotion the way principal dancer Irina Dvorovenko does. In the following pages, Alexandra gets to experience a taste of her dream, channeling ABT legend Nina

Ananiashvili and dancing with Maxim Belotserkovsky and Ethan Stiefel, two of the ABT's finest.

As for me, the dream did come true. I became a princess and I danced all over the world's stages. I danced with many famous people including Mikhail Baryshnikov, who was the director of American Ballet Theatre. He believed in me and was my mentor. Performing with Mischa was one of the most thrilling things in my life. Whenever he was onstage the atmosphere would change—to dance with someone so great made us all better dancers.

Just to be onstage is a dream fulfilled. By the time you are onstage performing for the audience, you have done all of your hard work to prepare for this moment. You have become your role. If you are dancing *Swan Lake*'s Swan Queen, you have rehearsed for at least two months every day, and you know her as well as you know yourself. You have gone to class every day to perfect

"My dream," says
Alexandra, "is to dance
*Swan Lake* like Nina
Ananiashvili. Her line
is so beautiful."

your movements, to learn where you need work, to jump higher, turnout further, lengthen every position until it is flawless. You have prepared dozens upon dozens of pointe shoes and worn them all out. You have spent hours in rehearsal until you feel like you cannot dance anymore. You've tried on your costume and learned where to set your gaze during the performance. And now is finally the moment. Your job is to tell a story and the responsibility of telling that story lies in the way that you move. And when you are done, it's time to take a bow. For whether you are dancing in Paris for royalty or in Maryland for your family, you are now what you have dreamed you would be: a ballerina.

84

DREAMING...

"Or maybe I'd partner
with Ethan Stiefel, who
would lift me as he did
his partner in *Romeo and
Juliet*—maybe even higher!"

BECOMING A BALLERINA

DREAMING...

BECOMING A BALLERINA

"Maxim Belotserkovsky
would lift me and I'd
gracefully look out at
the audience."

BECOMING A BALLERINA

"And when it was time for
the curtain call, everyone
would cheer!"

91

92

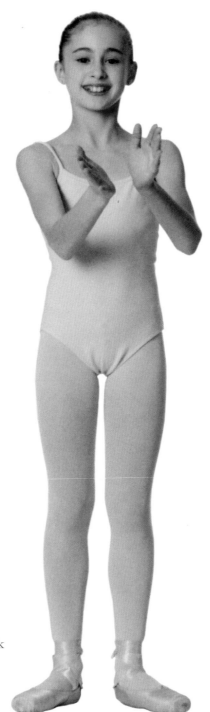

" To become a ballerina
is a dream come true,
made true with hard work
and lots of practice. But
there's nothing I would
rather be doing!"

DREAMING...

I want to thank Susan Jaffe for bringing her
style, elegance, and lovely memories of dance to our project.
Alexandra Dobles and Lexa Harpel were charming subjects,
and I'd like to thank them for being so hardworking.
Thank you also to Liz Kehler and Mary Jo Ziesel for finding
our young dancers and to Olga Dvorovenko for being
this project's ballet mistress.

We used the American Ballet Theatre's studios,
and it was our happy fortune that some of the ABT's principal
dancers dropped by to lend their talent: Irina Dvorovenko,
Maxim Belotserkovsky, and Ethan Stiefel—thank you!
My thanks also to Susan Jaffe, Ashley Tuttle, and Nina Ananiashvili, also
pictured in the book. Working with all of these incredible stars
is always a joy for me, and I thank them
for just being!

Capezio provided the wardrobe and shoes,
Green Rhino the prints, and Abby Bennett and John Klotnia
at Opto Design were the book's talented designers.
My very special thanks to everyone at Universe who brought
such care and attention to every detail.
Holly Rothman brought both her adult editorial skills and
her little-girl sensibilities to every aspect of our book's creation.
Thank you to Rebecca Cremonese, for the care
she put into the book's production. Finally, thank you
to my publisher, Charles Miers (and to his daughter, who surely
made a book like ours seem important to her dad).
It's hard to imagine the time and care it takes to bring a book
to publication and I thank you for caring so much.
—Nancy Ellison

I would like to thank Nancy Ellison for her friendship,
her spirit, and her inspiration in envisioning this book.
I would also like to thank my editor Holly Rothman
for her talent and her never-ending energy and enthusiasm.
A special thanks to Deborah Prutzman
for "being there" and to her partner Joel Scharfstein
for his generous help when I didn't
know where to turn.
—Susan Jaffe

95